Faithin' it:
THE RIDE

WHERE EVERY TWIST HAS A PURPOSE. EVERY DROP HAS A LESSON. EVERY UPHILL CLIMB LEADS TO SOMETHING GREATER– EVEN WHEN YOU'RE STILL IN THE MIDDLE OF IT. BUCKLE UP AND ENJOY THE RIDE.

alicia herring

FAITHIN' IT: THE RIDE
Scripture References & Permissions
Unless otherwise noted, all Scripture quotations are taken from the Holy Bible, New International Version® (NIV®). Copyright © 1973, 1978, 1984, 2011 by Biblica, Inc.™ Used by permission. All rights reserved worldwide. Scripture quotations marked ESV are from the ESV® Bible (The Holy Bible, English Standard Version®), Copyright © 2001 by Crossway, a publishing ministry of Good News Publishers. Used by permission. All rights reserved. Scripture quotations marked KJV are from the King James Version. Public domain. Scripture quotations marked AMP are from the Amplified® Bible, Copyright © 2015 by The Lockman Foundation. Used by permission. All rights reserved. www.lockman.org

ISBN - 979-8-218-68418-1

Published by: She Blooms Co.

introduction!

I had no idea this would turn into a devotional.

I just knew that when we got the call, I needed to get the thoughts out of my head. It was the only way I knew how to process it all without spilling it on anyone else. I didn't have a plan. I just knew I had to write.

But what started as raw, messy, daily journaling quickly turned into something more.

Because somewhere in the middle of the chaos, the confusion, the constant back and forth... God started writing with me. He was in the tears, the prayers, the breakdowns, and the breakthroughs. And I realized this wasn't just my story—
it was His.

His faithfulness.
His redirection.
His peace.
His protection.

This isn't a devotional about a destination.
It's about transformation.

About what happens when obedience doesn't lead to the outcome you expected, but still leads to the growth you didn't know you needed.

So if you find yourself journaling your own mess, know this: God isn't just watching your story—He's writing it with you.

Buckle up. Welcome to the ride.

To my family,

Thank you for riding this rollercoaster with me. For putting up with the stress, the mood swings, and all the "what ifs" along the way. I'm sorry for what I said when I was stressed. HA!

To my kids—you guys were troopers. Even when this felt more like a free-fall than a ride, you kept me going. You didn't want to move to Alabama (and, you made that clear!), but your honesty, resilience, and heart carried me more than you'll ever know. You are the reason I kept going on the days I wanted to quit. Thank you for being my why.

And to my husband, Ben—the one who took the scariest leap. You moved to a place with no family, no friends, and no guarantees, trusting God would meet you there. You wrestled with obedience and grew through it. Watching you step out in faith stirred something in me, too. I'm proud of you—more than I've ever said out loud.

This season stretched our faith, tested our peace, and taught us hard lessons. But we walked it out together, and that's what I'll remember most.

I love ya'll more than you'll ever know.

To Wendy:

You may never fully know what your prayers sparked, but I do. April a year ago, you sat with me in my dining room, whispered a prayer of deliverance, and as I hugged you through tears, a shadowed 7 appeared on the brick outside. We giggled as you just simply said, "It is complete!" I didn't fully understand it then—still don't—but I knew something had shifted.

And then there was that voice clip where you said you kept seeing the word HUB while praying for me—the very place God planted us for this season. A "HUB" City... You couldn't shake Esther 4:14: "And who knows whether you have not come to the kingdom for such a time as this?"

Now, as I finish this devotional, that same 7 has shown up again—almost a year to the day. God's just showing off!

Thank you for being the kind of friend who shows up, prays the bold prayers, and reminds me to keep saying yes, even when I can't see the end of the ride. This wouldn't exist without you.

Love you big.

"For I know the plans I have for you," declares the Lord, "plans to prosper you and not to harm you, plans to give you a hope and a future."

JEREMIAH 29:11 NIV

The First Click Up

"For I know the plans I have for you," declares the Lord, "plans to prosper you and not to harm you, plans to give you a hope and a future." Jeremiah 29:11 NIV

There are moments in life that feel exactly like that first click up on a rollercoaster. You're strapped in, unsure of what's ahead, inching upward one slow, jerky tug at a time—your stomach's already nervous and your mind's racing with every "what if." You know there's no turning back, but you still can't quite see what's on the other side of the climb.

That's where I found myself when this all began. My husband had just received a call about a life-altering job opportunity, and my world started to tilt. The fear of the unknown crept in hard—How will our kids react? Are we really considering this? What will this change mean for our family?

And then, there was P28.

A prayer initiative our church does every February— 28 days, one minute a day, at 1 p.m., praying for one specific thing.

This year? My husband's P28 prayer was this:

"God, show me where You want me to be—not where I want to be."

Whew. Be careful what you pray for, ya'll!

That line has echoed in every decision since.
It set this whole journey in motion. It was the first click up the track.
And here we are.
It hasn't been easy. But I'm learning that sometimes, when God is leading you somewhere, He won't show you the whole blueprint up front. He'll just give you the peace to take the first step. And then the next. And then the next.
So today, that's what I'm doing. Trusting Him in the unknown. Believing that even when the ride feels uncertain, He's the One steering the cart.

Reflect

What are the fears or uncertainties you're facing right now? How can you trust God in the midst of the unknown?

Faith Step

Take a moment today to sit in silence before God. Don't try to figure it all out—just sit with Him and say, "Lord, I don't know what to do, but I trust that You do." Let peace replace panic, even if only for a moment. That moment is where trust begins.

_____

_____

_____

_____

_____

_____

_____

Prayer

Lord, I ask for Your peace to fill my heart in this season of uncertainty. Help me to trust that You have a plan for our family, even when the path ahead isn't clear. Give me the courage to step forward with faith, knowing You are guiding us every step of the way. Amen.

Hold On Tight

"Trust in the Lord with all your heart and lean not on your own understanding; in all your ways submit to Him, and He will make your paths straight." Proverbs 3:5-6 NIV

This season is proving to be one giant emotional rollercoaster.

One minute I feel like I'm about to lose my lunch, and the next I'm whispering, "God's got this," like a mantra I desperately need to believe. The fear and uncertainty are real. I'm anxious about how our kids will respond to such a big shift, and I can't stop the swirl of "what ifs" in my mind.

But then I pause. I breathe. And I remember—God is good.

He opens doors on purpose. And sometimes those doors lead to even greater things we couldn't have dreamed up ourselves. The hard part? Trusting Him before we know the outcome. That's where the tension lives—between what we can see and what He already knows.

As I've told my husband for years, "You can't worry and trust God at the same time."

And now? I have to take my own advice. I'm standing in the middle of the unknown, wanting so badly to trust, but feeling the pull of fear. It's not easy to loosen your grip when everything feels uncertain. But obedience starts with one small step. Even when your heart is pounding. Even when you want to slam the brakes. Right now, I'm choosing to hold on tight—because even if I don't know what's coming, I know Who's with me in it.

Reflect

What emotions are you wrestling with today? How can you trust God with the next step, even when you don't know what's ahead?

Faith Step

Write down one specific fear that's been pulling at you today—especially one related to the unknown. Then, next to it, write: "God, I trust You more than this." It doesn't have to feel true yet. Just let your faith speak louder than your fear—even for a moment.

_____

_____

_____

_____

_____

_____

_____

Prayer

Lord, it's hard to trust right now. My heart is filled with fear and uncertainty, but I choose to lean on You and Your promises. Help me to take each step with faith, trusting that You are guiding us and that You know what's best. Amen.

The Trial Run

"Trust in the Lord with all your heart and lean not on your own
understanding; in all your ways submit to Him, and He will make
your paths straight." Proverbs 3:5-6 NIV

The weight of worry for our kids, wondering how
they'll handle this possible change, is heavy on my
heart. They'd be leaving friends behind, stepping into
the unknown, and that's a lot for them to carry—
especially when we don't even know if this is
permanent.

My own fears have been piling up too—about what's
ahead, about where we'll end up, about whether this
is really where God wants us. I keep thinking, "What if
this doesn't work out? What if this isn't it?"

But then I hear that whisper of truth: "What if it
doesn't work out... but darling, what if it does?"

And honestly? That's where we are right now. A trial
period. We don't have a permanent answer. There's a
chance we could return. And while that option offers
some comfort, it doesn't erase the fear of walking this
out in real time.

But faith isn't about guarantees—it's about trusting
anyway. It's about saying yes without a full picture.
It's about believing that if God opened this door, He's
already ahead of us on the other side.

This might not be the forever plan. But it's the next
step. And faith says, step anyway.

Reflect

What "what ifs" are holding you back from stepping forward in faith? How can you trust that God is guiding your next steps, even when the future seems uncertain?

Faith Step

Acknowledge the weight of your worry today. Write it down. Name it. Then ask God: "What do You want me to do with this?" Sometimes surrender is the step. Sometimes it's action. But always—obedience leads to peace.

_____

_____

_____

_____

_____

_____

_____

Prayer

Lord, I'm holding on to so many fears and questions, and I need Your peace. Help me to release my grip on the "what ifs" and trust that You've already gone ahead of us. Give me the faith to believe that even when I don't understand, You are in control. I choose to trust in You today and take the next step, no matter how unknown it may seem. Amen.

Hands in the Air

"Cast all your anxiety on him because he cares for you."
1 Peter 5:7 NIV

I've had moments in this journey—moments where I've stood in my closet, hands open, tears falling—whispering, "God, I can't do this anymore."
Not out of drama. Out of desperation.
Right now, it feels like everything is on my heart and mind all at once. The fear of the unknown. The pressure to make the "right" decision. The weight of what this means for our family. I've carried it all like it's my job—like if I hold it tightly enough, maybe I can fix it.
But God keeps reminding me: This isn't mine to carry.
The uncertainty, the fear, the "what ifs"—they don't belong to me. They belong to Him.
So today, I'm choosing to surrender.
Not because it's easy, but because it's the only way forward.
There's always that moment—when your stomach's in your throat, your grip is slipping, and you realize...
you're not in control of any of this. The drop's coming whether you're ready or not.

You just have to throw your hands in the air and trust the One who's got you strapped in... even if you're praying He double-checked the seatbelt.
I'm asking for peace.
For clarity.
For courage to take the next step—even if it feels like I'm free-falling with no backup plan and no control.
I trust Him in the silence.
I trust Him in the chaos.
And I trust Him with the outcome, even when I can't see what's on the other side of this hill... or if I'm about to scream the whole way down.

Reflect

What are you holding on to that you need to surrender today? How can you trust God with the next step, even when you can't see where it leads?

Faith Step

When you're staring down the unknown, repeat this promise over your heart: "Just because it's hard doesn't mean it's wrong." Say it every time fear tries to tell you otherwise. Obedience doesn't always make sense—but it always makes a way.

_____

_____

_____

_____

_____

_____

_____

_____

Prayer

Lord, I lay my fears and burdens at Your feet today. Help me to trust You with the unknowns and take the next step with faith. I surrender my worry, knowing that You are in control and that Your plan is always good. Guide me through this journey, step by step. Amen.

Thought We Were Getting Off Here

"And my God will meet all your needs according to the riches of his
glory in Christ Jesus." Philippians 4:19 NIV

Yesterday, my husband made the difficult decision to
turn down the job offer—an opportunity that promised
more financial freedom for our family. But the cost?
Potentially uprooting our kids from everything they
know and love. That just didn't sit right.
The thought of making them leave their friends, their
routines, and the only place they've ever called home—
for the sake of a paycheck—felt selfish.
Understandable, yes. But still... hard to reconcile.
So, we said no.
At least for now.
We made that decision with heavy hearts but total
trust—believing that if this wasn't it, God would still
provide. That His provision wouldn't hinge on one
offer or one move. That He would meet us in the
middle of our obedience and make a way.
And maybe that's what this was all about.
Maybe this wasn't the opportunity for this season.
Maybe it was a test of trust.
Or maybe it was a door God opened just to show us
He's not done opening them.

Closed doors are hard. Especially when you don't fully understand why. But I've come to believe that sometimes a closed door is the clearest form of protection. And sometimes, what we call a decision is actually just part of the process.
I don't have all the answers. And honestly? I'm starting to realize I don't need them.
Because I trust the One who is the answer.
God is our ultimate provider. And whether this was the "final decision" or not... He's still leading us, step by step.

Reflect

Have you ever had to make a hard choice that didn't seem to make sense at the time? How can you trust God with the closed doors and missed opportunities, knowing that He has a plan for your good?

Faith Step

Think of a closed door in your life that still feels a little raw. Instead of questioning why it closed, ask God to show you what He protected you from—or what He's preparing instead. Write a sentence of thanks for that door, even if it still stings.

_____

_____

_____

_____

_____

_____

_____

Prayer

Lord, I don't always understand why You close doors or why some opportunities pass us by, but I trust that You are always working for our good. Help me to embrace Your provision and trust that You will always take care of us, no matter what decisions we face. I rest in the confidence that You are our provider, and You will guide us through each step. Amen.

Click... Click... Wait

"There is a time for everything, and a season for every activity under the heavens." Ecclesiastes 3:1 NIV

Well... at the time, it felt like the right choice. But the peace? It just wasn't there.

Fear and uncertainty crept in—fear about the future, fear of disappointing our kids, fear of the unknown.

And when I tell you my husband couldn't sleep... oh my. It was a whole thing.

Now we're in a place of questioning: Is it "our doing" if he reaches back out and asks for more time? The decision window was so short, we barely had time to breathe—much less process and pray as a family.

We don't want to act out of panic.

We want to follow peace.

We want to follow Him.

What keeps running through my mind is the prayer my husband prayed for P28 this year—the same prayer he prayed five years ago when he started his job here (umm... wow, God).

"God, show me where You want me to be—not where I want to be."

That one line stopped me in my tracks. Because that's it. That's the heart behind everything we're walking through. Surrendering our plans. Releasing our expectations. Waiting on His direction—not our own desires.

But what if reaching back out isn't forcing something... What if it's part of the following?

What if this is how we seek clarity, wait on His answer, and trust that He's in the middle of all of it?

I'm learning—again—that we don't have to control the situation. We don't have to have it all figured out.

We just have to trust His timing, even when the path ahead is foggy.

Because He's got it covered.

Reflect

Do you find yourself questioning whether you're acting on your own or trusting God's timing? How can you let go of the pressure to figure everything out and trust that God will guide each step?

Faith Step

When clarity feels impossible, ask God for peace instead. Write down this prayer and memorize it: "God, if this is not Your plan, shut the door completely. And if it is, open it in a way only You can." Then breathe. Wait. And trust that no action on your part can override His will.

_____

_____

_____

_____

_____

_____

_____

Prayer

Lord, I'm struggling with the uncertainty of this decision and asking for Your wisdom. Help me to trust Your timing, knowing that You have a purpose for every season. If we need to ask for more time, guide us in that process. I place this all in Your hands, trusting that You'll make a way when the time is right. Amen.

Stuck at the Top

"Don't worry about anything. Instead, pray about everything with
thanksgiving, and God's peace will guard your heart and mind in
Christ." Philippians 4:6-7 NIV

After saying no to the job offer and still feeling
conflicted, he reached back out to see if we could at
least look at the place.
I mean, it makes sense, right?
If you're going to move a family of five, maybe it's a
good idea to actually visit the town first.
Maybe get a little clarity.
HA! Yeah right.
Dothan, Alabama. a HUB city...
We went.
We saw.
We survived.
And somehow, the weight of the decision was still just
as heavy.
He's gone back and forth, never finding peace either
way.
It's like he can't fully lean into taking the job, but he
also can't fully settle into letting it go.
Maybe it's just not the right opportunity for him in this
season.
Maybe it's something bigger we can't see yet.

All I know is this:
I'm praying for peace.
Real-unshakable peace.
Whether the answer is yes or no.
Whether we move or stay.
Because peace isn't tied to the place.
It's tied to the One who leads us there.
And right now, that's what I'm holding onto.

Reflect

Are you in a place of indecision or uncertainty? How can you ask God for peace, trusting that He will guide you through even the hardest decisions?

Faith Step

If you're in a back-and-forth season, give yourself permission to pause. Not to overthink—but to pray. Find a quiet space and whisper: "God, I'm listening. Show me Your peace in the midst of my confusion." Let His stillness speak louder than your stress.

_____

_____

_____

_____

_____

_____

_____

_____

Prayer

Lord, the stress and confusion are overwhelming, and I pray for peace in the midst of this uncertainty. I ask that You help my husband see You in this decision and that You bring clarity and peace to his heart. If this opportunity isn't right for us in this season, help us to accept that with peace and trust in Your perfect plan. Guard our hearts and minds as we navigate this journey. Amen.

"When you pass through the waters, I will be with you; and when you pass through the rivers, they will not sweep over you."

ISAIAH 43:2 NIV

The Emotional Loop-de-Loop

"So do not fear, for I am with you; do not be dismayed, for I am your God. I will strengthen you and help you; I will uphold you with my righteous right hand." Isaiah 41:10 NIV

My husband made the decision to turn down the job offer, and I was proud of him for making a choice that felt right for our family.

But then—because why not keep the rollercoaster going—he texted me, "I'm still not 100% sure."

Jesus, take the wheel.

The back and forth is playing with my emotions—one minute he felt peace, and the next he was second-guessing everything. It was exhausting. I was exhausted. And honestly, it started to feel like we were stuck in one giant emotional loop-de-loop.

After he turned it down, I thought we were done. Decision made. Done.

But about an hour later, he came across a post I had shared without thinking much about it:

"In the end, we only regret the chances we didn't take. Trust yourself, make the leap and create the life you deserve."

He sent it to me, and the second I saw it, I realized it hit him hard.

It was almost as if the quote spoke straight to the very decision he had just made.

He had talked himself out of the leap, and now he was stuck wrestling—not so much with the job itself, but with the fear underneath it.

Because fear?
Fear has a way of sneaking in and confusing everything, especially when the stakes are high. Fear of the unknown, fear of disappointing others, fear of making the wrong move—it's loud, it's convincing, and it drowns out the clarity we so desperately need.
But here's what I'm clinging to: if God opened this door, He will open another one—and maybe even one that's better than we could have imagined.
Are you exhausted yet, friend? Because I am.
The process is tough. The emotions are spinning like the tilt-a-whirl at a county fair. But even in the dizziness of it all, I'm choosing to believe that God's hand is steady, that He's still guiding us even when it feels like we're upside down and can't tell which way is up.

Reflect

Are you in a season where you feel like you're being called to step out of your comfort zone? How can you trust God, even when the path ahead is unclear?

Faith Step

What's one "God moment" that hit you unexpectedly this week—a post, a quote, a lyric? Write it down somewhere you can revisit. Then pray, "God, thank You for speaking even when I'm unsure if I'm hearing You right. Keep showing up—I'll keep watching."

_____

_____

_____

_____

_____

_____

_____

Prayer

Lord, stepping out in faith is hard, especially when I don't know what's next. But I trust that You will lead the way. Help me to release my grip on control and trust You with every step, even when the details aren't clear. Strengthen my faith in the waiting and guide me through the discomfort. Amen.

The Loop That Led to the Leap

"In the same way, faith by itself, if it is not accompanied by action, is dead." James 2:17 NIV

This has been the longest 12 days of my life. And, yes, I realize this is only day 9... Because some days I just can't.

The back-and-forth. The questions. The mental loops. It has been nonstop—like being strapped into a ride that keeps climbing, dropping, twisting, and jerking you in every direction before you can catch your breath.

I can't make this up, y'all... this morning, he asked me again, "Should I take it?" At that point, I was like, "Okay, Jesus, just take the whole car!"

I ran straight to the closet to pray because I didn't even know what to say. I just sat there, broken and desperate for clarity. And then it came—so clearly in my spirit: "Do you think this is being disobedient?"

I got up, calmly off the floor, and right about then my phone rang. It was him: "Did you see my text?" Um, YES. But I needed to go talk to Jesus about it first! I knew right then—that was the question I had to ask him. If we were turning it down out of fear—if we were clinging to comfort instead of walking in faith—then the next step was obvious. We had to trust. We had to say yes. Even without all the answers.

I asked him, and without hesitation, he said yes. And I just stood there like, Well... you know what you have to do now. After more prayer, more pacing, and more conversations, he took the job. The very one we'd gone back and forth on for days. He said yes. And it felt heavy and holy all at once.
I still have no idea how all of this is going to unfold. But this time? There's peace. No more sleepless nights about what to do—only the preparation for how we're going to walk it out. He's ready. He's eager. And I'm honestly just grateful. I may still be holding my breath a little (let's be real), but I know now: something shifted the moment we chose obedience over comfort.
That kind of faith feels shaky at first... until you realize He's already gone ahead of you.

Reflect

How is fear influencing your decisions right now? What would it look like to trust God with the next step, even if it feels uncertain?

Faith Step

Think about a moment recently when you felt like you talked yourself out of something because of fear. Write it down. Now ask God: "Was I disobedient... or just scared?" Invite Him to show you if that decision needs to be revisited—or released.

_____

_____

_____

_____

_____

_____

_____

_____

Prayer

Lord, I know fear has a way of clouding our judgment and creating confusion. I ask that You bring clarity and peace to our hearts, and help us trust that You are leading us to the right path. Thank You for guiding us, even when we don't have all the answers. Amen.

Off the Rails and Overwhelmed

"Come to me, all you who are weary and burdened, and I will give you rest." Matthew 11:28 NIV

This has been one of the hardest things I've ever walked through. Emotionally, I'm drained. Worn out. Unwell. I've carried the weight of my kids' emotions, my husband's wrestling, my friends' struggles—and somewhere in the middle of it all, I forgot to check in with me.

I've been trying to be strong for everyone else, holding it together so no one else breaks. I've held back how I really feel because I don't want to add more stress to Ben. But inside? I need rest. I need peace. I need a break from carrying weight that was never mine to carry in the first place.

And here's what I'm learning:

I don't have to be the strong one. That's God's job.

I don't have to carry everyone's burdens. He already carried them to the cross.

I don't have to pretend I'm okay. My feelings are valid. My heart matters too.

It's time to pray. To surrender. To trust. Not in my ability to hold it all together... but in His ability to hold me together when I feel like I'm unraveling.

And even in the mess, even when the rollercoaster feels like it's never gonna end—I see a light. Ben is happy. He's thriving. He's stepping into this new role, and it's not just a job—it's a place where I can already see God growing him in ways we didn't even know needed growing. And even though I'm still tired, even though my emotions are somewhere between "hang on tight" and "please make it stop," I know I'm growing too.

Maybe that's the thing about faith… You're flying through a dark tunnel, holding your breath, scared out of your mind— and then out of nowhere, you see it. Just a tiny crack of light.

Just enough to remind you: you're not stuck. You're not alone. You're getting through this.

So today? I'm letting go. Laying it down. Choosing rest over striving, peace over pressure, and trust over trying to control what was never mine to carry.

Even if it feels like I blacked out somewhere along the way—I know the same God who met me in the dark will carry me straight through to the light.

Reflect

Have you been carrying burdens that don't belong to you?
What would it look like to release them into God's hands
and receive His rest today?

Faith Step

If you've been running scenarios in your head, pause and
ask this question: "God, is this fear or obedience?" Jot
down what you feel in your spirit. And if you sense He's
nudging you toward something, even if it's uncomfortable,
take one small step that direction today.

_____

_____

_____

_____

_____

_____

_____

_____

Prayer

Father, I'm tired. I've been carrying things You never asked
me to carry. Help me to surrender it all to You—the fears,
the pressure, the responsibility. I need Your rest. Remind me
that I don't have to be strong for everyone else, because
You are my strength. Thank You for loving me in my
weakness. Amen.

The Pause Before the Plunge

"The Lord is close to the brokenhearted and saves those who are
crushed in spirit." Psalm 34:18 NIV

Some days, just getting out of bed feels like a victory.
Some days, it's a win if you brush your teeth or put
on something other than your softest cardigan.
And other days?
You just sit there.
In your emotions, in your numbness, in your pajamas.
You're here—but barely.
That's today for me. And I'm learning that here is still
a place where God meets me.
I don't do life well when it's hard.
I retreat.
I shut down.
I turn off the noise because everything feels too loud.
But today, I texted friends for prayer. I opened my
Bible app. I didn't have words, but I searched for His.
I think that's enough for today.
That's my obedience in this moment.
Searching for what God wants to say in the middle of
emotional exhaustion, feeling buried beneath the
weight I keep trying to carry.

Ben and I have told the kids we're going to keep everything as normal as possible.

Dance tryouts, cheer fittings, spring basketball—all of it.

We don't know what next week holds, much less five months from now, but we do know this: we want to give them stability where we can. We want to honor their "right now," even while praying through the possibility of a different future.

And I'll rest today. And I'll believe He'll speak.

Maybe through a devotional, maybe through a nap, maybe through the silence.

But He'll speak. Because He always does.

Reflect

What small act of obedience can you take today—just to be still, just to show up? Where might God want to meet you in your "just here" moments?

Faith Step

Search the Word. Literally. Go to your Bible app, pick a word that reflects your emotional state (like rest, overwhelmed, or burdened)—and let God speak through His Word. Write down the first verse that hits your spirit. That's your anchor for today.

_____

_____

_____

_____

_____

_____

_____

Prayer

Lord, I'm here. I don't feel strong, I don't feel inspired, I barely feel anything at all. But I'm showing up anyway. Meet me in this space. Speak to me in ways only You can. I'm tired, I'm weary, and I just need You. Amen.

The Drop You Can't See

"Have I not commanded you? Be strong and courageous. Do not be afraid; do not be discouraged, for the Lord your God will be with you wherever you go." Joshua 1:9 NIV

This.is.hard.

Like, soul-aching, heart-heavy, mind-spinning kind of hard.

I'm watching my daughter pour her heart into dance—she's talking about tryouts, summer camp, practices—and I'm carrying the unbearable thought that she may not even get to dance next year. The possibility of pulling her away from her friends, her passion, her normal… it's wrecking me.

How are we even considering this?

And it's not just her.

My kids don't want to move. They don't want to leave the life they know.

And I can't blame them.

I'm trying to be strong, but right now? I'm not. I'm overwhelmed.

And honestly? I'm tired of pretending I'm okay.

I can't carry this alone. And I was never meant to.

But even in the middle of this emotional rollercoaster, I know one thing: obedience is the next step.

I don't have to have the whole plan laid out.
I don't even need to know the outcome.
I just need to take the next step. And for me, that next step—however scary—is touring the schools.
The step I've avoided.
The one I've tiptoed around because of fear.
Fear of my kids being mad at me.
Fear of their hearts breaking.
Fear of being "the bad guy" for leading our family into something unknown.
But God didn't give me a spirit of fear—He calls me to be fearless because He's with me.
Right now, fearless doesn't look loud or bold.
It looks like one shaky, surrendered step at a time...
Trusting that He's already gone before me.

Reflect

Is fear keeping you from taking the next step? What would it look like to move forward in obedience—even if your heart feels fragile?

Faith Step

If solitude has felt more like a sentence than a sanctuary, it's time to bring that into the light. Open your hands—physically if you can—and pray, "God, I can't keep holding this alone." Then write a short note or text to someone safe. Let them see you.

_____

_____

_____

_____

_____

_____

_____

_____

Prayer

God, I'm scared. I'm overwhelmed. And I feel so heavy with the weight of what this means for my family. But I know that You are leading us. Give me the courage to take the next step, even if it's scary. Remind me that obedience isn't about having it all together—it's about trusting You enough to follow. Hold our hearts and guide our steps. Amen.

The Heart-Drop

"Trust in the Lord with all your heart and lean not on your own understanding." Proverbs 3:5 NIV

Today, it's Brody.
Yesterday it was LC.
Tomorrow? I don't even know. All I know is this hurts in a way I can't explain.
We took the whole family out yesterday, and Brody brought his girlfriend—this precious, kind, sweet girl who has woven her way into his heart and ours.
And the thought of moving him 5.5 hours away from her? It's wrecking me.
What kind of parent does that?
What kind of mom even considers it?
I feel like I'm destroying their world—their friendships, their relationships, their memories—and somewhere deep down, I start to wonder if they'll ever forgive us for even thinking about this.
It's one thing to trust God with your own life.
It's another to trust Him with your kids' hearts.
Honestly?
It feels like we were climbing toward hope... and suddenly, the bottom dropped out.

I've never questioned God like this before.
Why are we even in this position?
Why are we being asked to make a decision that feels like it tears us in half?
Why does obedience hurt so bad?
I don't have the answers. I don't know the why.
But somewhere in the middle of the tears and the guilt and the ache, I hear a whisper:
You don't have to understand. You just have to trust Me.
So I'm trying.
I'm trying to trust that God is good, even when this doesn't feel good.
I'm trying to believe that His plan is still perfect, even when I feel like everything is unraveling.
And I'm trying to remember that grief and trust can coexist.

Reflect

Are you holding onto guilt, fear, or grief that feels too big
to carry? What would it look like to trust God with the
emotions you don't even have words for?

Faith Step

List the emotions that have been the loudest in your head
lately—sadness, guilt, anger, grief. Then beside each one,
write a truth about who God is. Let His identity reframe
your reality. You don't have to stuff the feelings—you just
don't have to stay stuck in them.

_____

_____

_____

_____

_____

_____

_____

Prayer

God, I'm wrecked. I don't understand why this is happening
or what You're doing. I feel like I'm hurting my kids, and the
weight of that is unbearable. Please hold me through this.
Remind me that I don't have to have all the answers. Just
show me how to trust You, one breath at a time. I surrender
my guilt, my pain, and my questions to You. Lead me in love.
Amen.

The Longest Stretch

"Trust in the Lord with all your heart and lean not on your own
understanding." Proverbs 3:5 NIV

This is the part that no one really talks about—the in-
between.
The space where life looks normal, but your heart is
anything but.
We're going about our days, waking up, getting
dressed, showing up… while this huge, looming
possibility hovers in the background.
What do you do when everything feels normal now,
but you know that in a blink, everything might
change?
How do you look at your kids, knowing you may have
to uproot them from their school, their friends, their
routines—and say nothing yet because the decision
isn't final?
How do you function in the not-knowing?
We've already had to sit with hard conversations.
We've already felt the sting of thinking through what
it would look like for their dad to be 5.5 hours away.
Weeks without hugs.
And now we're back at it again—another step, another
conversation, this time about touring schools.
It feels like reopening a wound that hasn't even had
time to scab.

I wanted this to bring us closer as a family—not make us feel like we're coming undone.
But here's what I'm clinging to: the in-between is not wasted.
It's not a mistake.
It's a place where God meets us gently and quietly and says,
"You don't have to figure it all out. Just walk with Me today."
So today, I'll cry if I need to. I'll feel all of it.
But I'll also take the next step—even if my knees are shaking—because I trust that God is with us in the now and the not yet.

Reflect

Are you living in an in-between season? What would it look like to be still and trust God with today, even while tomorrow feels uncertain?

Faith Step

When the future feels fragile, focus on what you do know today. What's one thing you're grateful for in this exact moment? Name it. Then whisper this prayer: "God, thank You for this. I trust You with the rest." Repeat as needed. It's your breath prayer today.

_____

_____

_____

_____

_____

_____

_____

_____

Prayer

Lord, this in-between space is crushing at times. I feel stuck—like I'm living two lives: the one I know, and the one that might be. I need Your strength to walk this out. Help me not to rush ahead, but to walk with You step by step. Be near to our family as we navigate these conversations and decisions. Bring peace where there is fear, and unity where there is tension. Amen.

God is still writing your story. Don't give up on the chapter you're in.

The Breakdown in the Middle

By day the Lord went ahead of them in a pillar of cloud to guide them... and by night in a pillar of fire to give them light, so that they could travel by day or night." Exodus 13:21 NIV

I feel like Moses today.
Wandering. Weary. Crying out in the wilderness of my emotions.
It's hard to describe the weight pressing on my chest. I'm curled up on the couch in a fetal position, wearing the shirt my husband hugged me in this morning, and I can still smell his cologne. It's oddly comforting and completely undoing me at the same time.
I can't move.
I know I should—LC's car needs a tire looked at, I haven't showered, and Brody has something exciting starting soon. But all I can think is, "And here I am, possibly taking that away too."
I feel like I'm ruining it all.
Every opportunity. Every plan. Every comfort my kids have ever known.
And my face? It's a swollen, puffy mess from all the crying I've done trying to make sense of any of this.

I keep begging, "God, speak to me. Please. I need a billboard. A sign. A whisper. Anything."
But maybe the whisper isn't something external today.
Maybe it's the fact that I'm still showing up in this pain.
Maybe it's knowing that Moses wandered too… but he was never alone.
God was in the fire.
In the cloud.
In the silence.
And He's in this.
Even here.
Even now.
I don't have to have it together today.
I just have to keep letting Him lead—even if all I can do is crawl.

Reflect

Have you ever felt like you're wandering with no direction? What would it look like to trust that God is still leading you, even in the silence?

Faith Step

Take one brave action toward the unknown—no matter how small. Maybe it's researching something. Maybe it's just not avoiding it for once. Speak this over yourself as you do: "I'm not walking into this alone. God is already there."

_____

_____

_____

_____

_____

_____

_____

_____

Prayer

Lord, I feel lost. Tired. Paralyzed by the weight of what I'm carrying. Please speak to me. I need You more than ever. Help me trust that You haven't left me in this wilderness— that You're still guiding me, even if all I can see is the next breath. Be my strength today. Be my direction. Amen.

Through the Smoke and Mirrors

"We know God works all things together for the good of those who love Him and are called to His purpose." Romans 8:28 AMP

Today, I stumbled onto a word—or maybe it stumbled onto me.
If something grabs my attention, especially if it relates to the Word, I start digging. That's what growth looks like sometimes—chasing after what God might be trying to show you, even if you don't fully understand it at first.
And this word? I had never even heard it before.
Kairos.
As I started researching, it felt like a little nudge from Heaven—a whisper saying, "Pay attention. This is for you." That's when I found the phrases that hit me right in the heart:
"You are in a Kairos moment."
"This isn't chaos—it's divine transition."
Kairos isn't just another hard season. It's not more unknowns, exhaustion, or emotional storms.
Kairos is a divine moment in time. A shift. A window of strategic, God-ordained purpose.
(**Side note:** If you skipped the Note to Wendy...girl, you need to go back and read that. We talked about this shift almost a year ago.)

Maybe that's what this whole thing has been.
Maybe the grief, the fear, the questions—they're not just hurdles to survive.
Maybe they're the runway God is using to launch us into something we never saw coming.
Maybe this isn't the enemy winning.
Maybe it's God re-aligning.
And yet... the enemy is LOUD. He's using smoke and mirrors to distort what's real—making it look like everything is falling apart when really, something sacred is being rebuilt.
It's intimidating.
It's disorienting.
It's heartbreaking.
But it's not without purpose.
God said, "Speak to the smoke. Stand on what tried to knock you down. Keep your eyes on Me." And I'm doing just that.
Today, I don't need to have all the answers. I just need to remember that even in the swirl of confusion, I'm standing on holy ground.
This moment is not wasted.
This pain is not punishment.
This chaos? It's not chaos—it's divine transition.

Reflect

Are you letting fear and uncertainty paint a false picture of what God is doing? What if the very thing that feels like opposition is actually the launching pad for your next season?

Faith Step

Let yourself feel. Don't rush to "fix it" or force the positive spin. Instead, journal the sentence: "God, I don't like this, but I still believe You're good." Then breathe. Sometimes honesty is the obedience. Let Him meet you in the middle of it.

_____

_____

_____

_____

_____

_____

_____

Prayer

Lord, I'm listening. I see the smoke and I feel the pressure, but I'm choosing to believe You are working. Remind me that this is a Kairos moment. Turn what feels like opposition into momentum. Help me see what's real—what's Yours—and silence the lies. Thank You for speaking so clearly. I trust You. Amen.

Divine Road Signs

"Call to me and I will answer you and tell you great and unsearchable things you do not know." Jeremiah 33:3

It started with numbers.

Not just once, not just randomly, but so intentionally that it felt too specific to ignore.

My husband was sitting in a meeting, and suddenly, numbers started popping up in ways that felt too strategic to brush off. 111... 555. At first, it almost seemed silly. But deep down, my spirit knew—it wasn't random. It was confirmation. It was conversation. It was God saying, "Look closer. I'm in this."

And honestly? It felt like spotting a huge sign flashing ahead when you're climbing that first hill on a rollercoaster—not to scare you, but to steady you. A reminder that even when the ride feels shaky, He's already gone before you.

Here's what I've come to understand about the numbers God uses to get my attention:

111 is about alignment. A divine nudge. It's God whispering, "I'm here. Stay close. I'm aligning things even when it feels like you're free-falling." It's about unity, purpose, and new beginnings.

555 is about movement. Shift. (That word again!!) Transformation. It's Heaven's way of saying, "I'm shaking things up—not to wreck you, but to release you." Breakthrough. Acceleration. That jolt you feel right before the biggest part of the ride.

And the fact that both of those numbers showed up while my husband was sitting in a meeting that could change everything for our family? That wasn't a whisper. That was a megaphone.

And then came this verse: Jeremiah 33:3—God's hotline, His invitation: "Call to Me, and I will answer you. I'll show you what you can't see."

And now? I'm realizing that sometimes, God doesn't send confirmation because the thing will last forever. He sends it to give us permission to step out in obedience for a season.

The signs still mattered—even if they were only meant to carry us through a season.

The nudges, the numbers, the whispers—those were real.

Because confirmation isn't always about forever.

Sometimes, it's just about trusting Him enough to say yes—even when you can't see how it all plays out.

So now? I'm paying attention.

To the grace. The timing. The way He shows up when I need it most.

Because if God's speaking—I want to be the kind of girl who listens.

Reflect

Has God been showing up in ways you didn't expect? Are there signs, numbers, or moments you've been brushing off that could be His way of speaking?

Faith Step

Choose one thing today that usually drains you—and instead of carrying it silently, hand it over. Out loud. Say, "God, this is too much for me, but it's not too much for You." Then let it go, even if you have to keep letting it go again tomorrow.

_____

_____

_____

_____

_____

_____

_____

_____

Prayer

Lord, thank You for using the little things to send a big message. Help me to stay in tune with the ways You speak, even when it's not loud or obvious. Let me notice the numbers. Catch the whispers. And trust that You are aligning everything in perfect timing. Amen.

The Steady Climb

"Isaac planted crops in that land and the same year reaped a hundredfold, because the Lord blessed him." Genesis 26:12 NIV

I've been praying a very specific prayer for years now. Not just casually. Not just in a crisis. But consistently—deeply—from a place in my heart that fully believed God was listening: "Make me an Isaac to my generation as he was to his."

I used to pray, "Strengthen my faith," but somewhere along the ride, I realized—I'm already walking in it. I've been praying with faith. Living by it. Declaring what I couldn't yet see. And let me just say... if you start praying for something, you better be prepared for the tests to come—or for everything hidden to start being laid out whether you want it or not. (Ask me how I know. Ha!)

Just recently, I finally realized what I'd been asking for all along. Isaac wasn't loud. He wasn't flashy. (Let's be real—not like me the time I strolled into a blacklight pep rally wearing a purple shirt with neon yellow FAITH across the chest, completely clueless I was about to glow like a human highlighter. Walked in like, "Oh heyyyy!" IYKYK (that was a totally different level of flashy.)

Issac was steady. Obedient. Trusting. Blessed. He was the miracle baby—the fulfillment of God's promise. A man who walked in peace and reaped blessing because of it. He trusted when it made no sense. He obeyed even when it felt uncomfortable. And he reaped a hundredfold—not because everything was easy, but because God's favor rested on him.

That's what I've been praying for—without even fully realizing it. And now? I'm starting to see it. God's been answering that prayer all along—even through the bumps, blind curves, and rollercoaster loops I never saw coming. That prayer didn't just come from my mouth; it came from the deepest part of me that trusted Him, even when everything around me felt shaky.

I didn't always understand it. I didn't always feel it. And honestly? I kind of quit praying for "stronger faith" because I thought surely I had been tested enough. But God wasn't done growing me yet.

"Lord, I trust You to do the impossible. I receive Your promises. I'm not perfect, but I'm willing. Make me an Isaac."

And somehow, through all the ups, downs, twists, turns, and quiet climbs—He's been doing just that.

Reflect

What prayers have you been repeating for years? Could it be that God's been answering them all along, even in ways you haven't fully seen?

Faith Step

If your thoughts are spiraling, pause and whisper: "Peace be still." Say it again. And again. Let your soul settle under the weight of that promise. Then, physically do something small that brings you comfort—a blanket, a walk, a song—and invite God into that moment with you.

_____

_____

_____

_____

_____

_____

_____

_____

Prayer

Lord, make me an Isaac. I want to walk in the promises You've spoken, trust You when it doesn't make sense, and carry Your blessing into the world around me. Thank You for shaping me through every whisper and every wait. Even when I didn't understand, You were working. Let my life be a living testimony of Your faithfulness. Amen.

Faith in the Whiplash

"For God is not the author of confusion, but of peace…"
1 Corinthians 14:33 KJV

I feel like I have emotional whiplash most days. Every morning seems to come with new emotions, new questions, and not nearly enough answers. One day I think I'm standing on something solid, and the next—it's like the floor drops out from under me, and I'm left scrambling to find my footing all over again.

God isn't the author of confusion—I know that. I've clung to that truth. But when confusion is all I can see, I start to wonder what that really means. If God isn't writing this chapter, then who is?

Am I just missing the plot completely?

Here's what I've come to realize: confusion doesn't always mean you're lost. Sometimes it means you're in the middle of a transition. Kind of like when you're riding one of those rollercoasters that launches you backward up a hill—completely disoriented—only to sling you forward into something new. You don't feel steady. You don't feel certain. But you're still moving toward something.

It's a moment where your old way of seeing, knowing, and planning is being stripped away so you can lean on faith in a deeper way. It's uncomfortable. It's frustrating. And if I'm being totally honest, I'm still questioning God. And I hate that.

But even in my questioning, I still know this: His plan is good. It always has been. It always will be.
I just don't like this part of it.
I want clarity. I want direction. I want the next steps written out in bold ink.
Maybe even shoot me a text??
But God's like, Nope... I didn't ask you to understand it or like it—I asked you to trust Me.
Maybe you're there, too.
Standing somewhere between the drop and the next climb, holding on for dear life, trying to make sense of it all.
If that's you, I want to remind you:
Strip away the confusion, and what do you find?
Peace that doesn't make sense.
Hope that refuses to quit.
A quiet strength that says, "I don't get it—but I'll still go."
That's faith.
That's trust.
That's surrender in action.
Clarity might not be the gift today.
But peace can be.
Let go of the need to understand.
And lean into the One who already does.

Reflect

Where have I been demanding clarity from God instead of trusting Him step-by-step?

Faith Step

When clarity doesn't come, don't chase it—just chase God. Light a candle, play worship, or simply sit with Him and ask: "What's my next right step, Lord?" Write down whatever comes—even if it's just wait. That's a step, too.

_____

_____

_____

_____

_____

_____

_____

Prayer

Lord, I don't like this season of uncertainty. It feels messy and hard, and I'm tired of not knowing. But I choose to trust You, even when I don't understand. Help me surrender the need to control and replace my confusion with Your peace. You are not the author of confusion, so I place my swirling thoughts in Your hands. Lead me, even if all I can do is follow the sound of Your whisper. Amen.

"The Lord is near to the brokenhearted and saves the crushed in spirit."

PSALM 34:18 NIV

Fallout of Faith

"The Lord is near to the brokenhearted and saves the crushed in
spirit." – Psalm 34:18 ESV

There's a different kind of ache when you feel like you've been left standing in the fallout—alone. Not loud, not dramatic… just alone. The kind of alone where the silence gets heavy and the thoughts won't stop circling. Where your soul feels worn thin from carrying too much for too long.

I've been in protective mode lately—more than I want to admit. Guarding my heart. Guarding my mind. Guarding the life God has given me. And I know it's made me quieter, more cautious, maybe even a little distant. But it hasn't been fake. It's been necessary. Because behind the scenes, fear's been rising. Not just everyday fear—the crippling kind. The kind that shows up with all the "what ifs" you didn't ask for. The kind that weighs you down until you wonder if you even have the strength to keep trusting.

My mind has been spinning. The unknowns feel too big. And the truth is… I don't want to fall apart, so I've held everything in. Tightly. Quietly.

But even in the loneliness—even when it feels like no one else sees the battle—I know this: God sees what no one else does.
He sees my solitude.
He sees the weight I'm carrying.
He sees the fear I'm too exhausted to speak out loud.
And He meets me there—not with guilt or shame, but with comfort. Not with answers, but with His presence. Not with pressure, but with peace.
He's not asking me to solve it all.
He's just asking me to come to Him with it.

Reflect

Where have you been holding everything in lately? Have you confused your self-protection with strength? Where might God be inviting you to release what you've been carrying?

Faith Step

Take a moment, open your hands, and say: "God, I give You what I can't hold anymore." You don't have to list it all. He already knows. Just let Him have it.

_____

_____

_____

_____

_____

_____

_____

Prayer

God, I feel like I've been holding my breath—trying to stay strong when I'm anything but. I've been in survival mode, and I'm tired. I don't want to carry this fear or pretend I'm okay anymore. Meet me here—in the silence and the swirl of emotions. Remind me I'm not alone, not forgotten, not too much. You are near. You are my peace. Amen.

The Scariest Ride

"And we know that in all things God works for the good of those who love Him, who have been called according to His purpose." –
Romans 8:28 (NIV)

Today I made the call.
The one I've been putting off.
The one I've been dreading.
The one that made everything feel real.
I scheduled a tour for the school our kids might attend if we move.
And. I. Sobbed. Like, ugly cry.
Not because it's a done deal. Not because everything is settled. But because this one phone call cracked open a whole world of emotions I've been trying to keep together.
My heart aches for our kids—especially my oldest. Her dance team, her passion, her community, her people… they're everything to her. And this new school? It doesn't even have a dance team. I feel like I'm watching a door close on something she cherishes, and I want so badly to stop it.
I'm scared our kids will hate us.
I'm scared they'll be angry, hurt, or lost in the transition.
And honestly? I'm scared that even after all of this… it still might not work out.

I mean, let's be honest... It would almost be easier if my husband just said, "Pack up. We're going."
But he hasn't. Because he's unsure too. Because this isn't just a job—it's a life shift.
And none of us are totally confident in what it's supposed to look like.
So here I am—somewhere between broken and obedient.
Crying out to God, "I know this is the next step. I know You're asking us to move forward in faith. But Lord... this hurts. This is so heavy. And the fear is real."
It's not that I don't believe God's plan is good—I do. I believe it's better than anything we could plan for ourselves.
But that doesn't mean the journey doesn't wreck me.
Sometimes obedience doesn't look like bold confidence.
Sometimes it looks like shaking hands and tear-stained cheeks making a hard phone call because it's the next right thing.

Reflect

What step have you been putting off out of fear or uncertainty? Have you equated obedience with certainty when it might actually just mean movement?

Faith Step

Acknowledge the step you're afraid to take. Write it down. Pray over it. Then take just one move in that direction and trust that God will guide the rest.

_____

_____

_____

_____

_____

_____

_____

_____

Prayer

God, I did what You asked, but it hurts more than I expected. I'm grieving what could be lost and afraid of what's ahead. Still, I trust You. Hold my heart through what I can't understand. Give me peace where fear wants to rise. You are good. You are faithful. I'll keep walking with You. Amen.

Faith in Motion

"Trust in the Lord with all your heart and lean not on your own understanding; in all your ways submit to Him, and He will make your paths straight." – Proverbs 3:5-6 NIV

Sometimes we have to make grown-up decisions. Even the kind that feel heavy in all the worst ways. I made the call. Scheduled the family tour. Took that next step in obedience. But now…

Now comes the part that might be even harder: telling the kids.

It might not sound like much to someone else. But when you're a mama whose heart beats for her babies—who knows what they love, who they're becoming, what routines they cling to—it feels like breaking a piece of their world open with your bare hands. It feels like you become the disruption. The disappointment. The reason for their heartbreak.

And all I want to do is protect them from that.

But after praying and crying and walking through all the fear of what this means, this is what I keep hearing God say:

"Alicia, this is just the next step in obedience. You don't know what the future holds, but I do. And if you don't take the step, you won't see what I can do—not just for you, but for your kids. Show them what obedience looks like. Show them what I can do through it."

Nothing is final. We haven't made the move. But this? This is what faith looks like.

It's not always packing the boxes. Sometimes it's just having the conversation.

It's saying: "I don't know how this ends, but I know I need to take the next right step."

It's being honest with your children that this hurts you too—but God is still in it.

Because maybe this isn't about a school tour at all. Maybe it's about giving them front row seats to faith in motion.

Maybe it's about showing them what trust looks like when the road isn't paved and the destination isn't clear.

That's what I want them to see. That's what I want them to remember.

This is just one of those steps.

But it's one step that sets faith in motion.

And sometimes? That's exactly where the miracle begins.

Reflect

Who in your life needs to see your faith lived out—even if it's messy? How can you be honest and obedient at the same time?

Faith Step

Invite someone into the process. Don't just take the step alone—share what God is doing with the people walking it with you. Let your obedience be a living testimony.

_____

_____

_____

_____

_____

_____

_____

Prayer

God, I'm afraid to bring my kids into this conversation. I don't want to hurt them, and I'm scared of how they'll respond. But I know You're leading us, and I don't want to hold back when You've already spoken. Help me speak with love, clarity, and peace. Give my children ears to hear—not just me, but You. Let this moment be a seed of faith that grows in them, and a reminder to me that I don't walk this road alone. Amen.

"Many are the plans in a person's heart, but it is the Lord's purpose
that prevails." Proverbs 19:21 NIV

I had the text all typed out.
The message for my kids. The one that explained
what was happening, what we were walking through,
and how this school tour was just the next step in
obedience.
It was ready to go. Sitting there, waiting to be sent
after school.
I had prayed over it. Cried over it. Stood in it.
And not three hours later... the phone rang.
"I'm on my way home…"
And just like that—everything changed.
It felt exactly like one of those moments on a
rollercoaster where you think you're about to coast
into a smooth stretch... only to be whipped into a loop
you never saw coming.
Everything we were planning, praying over, preparing
for—paused.
Just like that.

I called the school and said we're holding off on the tour. Because honestly? We don't know what's next anymore.

And I could sit here and overanalyze it all—wondering if my obedience somehow fast-tracked this whole thing. Wondering if this was God's "See? This is what I'm doing" kind of moment.

But maybe it's not about figuring it out.

Maybe it's just another reminder that this story isn't mine to write.

God knows what He's doing. Even when we don't. Even when everything changes before we have time to process it.

So, here we are again.

Paused. Confused. Waiting.

But still believing He's working—especially when we can't see it.

Reflect

What's one step of obedience God has asked you to take that felt uncomfortable or unclear? How might your willingness to move forward—even without answers—be shaping someone else's faith?

Faith Step

If something unexpected has interrupted your plans, pause and ask: "God, what do You want to show me here?" Write down one way He might be protecting or redirecting you —not to make sense of it, but to remind your heart He's still in control.

_____

_____

_____

_____

_____

_____

_____

_____

Prayer

Lord, I didn't see this coming. I thought I was taking the right step, and now it feels like everything just flipped upside down again. I'm trying to stay faithful, but I'm also just... tired. Help me not to spiral. Remind me that Your plans haven't changed just because mine have. You are still good. Still in control. Still working. Even here. Amen.

The Fall Before the Rise

"The Lord is close to the brokenhearted and saves those who are
crushed in spirit." Psalm 34:18 NIV

I thought we were being obedient.
We prayed. We wrestled. We searched for peace—
and when we found it, we followed it.
Even when it was hard. Even when it didn't make
sense. Even when we had no clue what the outcome
would be.
And now… it feels like the whole thing just fell apart.
My husband quit today.
He walked away from the job that was supposed to
be life-changing.
And maybe it was—just not in the way we expected.
The stress. The heartbreak. The weight of it all.
It didn't just land heavy—it broke us in ways we didn't
see coming.
And now the question we didn't want to ask can't be
ignored: Was this the right thing for us?
Because the truth is… no paycheck is worth sacrificing
your peace.
No opportunity is worth losing the foundation God
has built in your family.
It's not that the job itself was wrong.
It's that the timing—and the toll it was taking on us—
wasn't right for this season.

Maybe someday, in a different season, there will be another opportunity.
But for now? We had to choose peace over pressure.
Obedience over obligation.
And while I still don't have the full picture of what God was doing, I do know this:
His plans are still good.
Even when they lead through pain.
Even when obedience hurts.
Maybe the blessing wasn't in what we tried to step into.
Maybe it was in being willing to step out—no matter the cost.
Maybe it wasn't about achieving something... but about becoming something.
About trusting Him when everything inside us wanted answers instead.
About walking forward even when it felt like walking blindfolded.
Because the real gift isn't clarity.
It's the growth that comes from doing the hard thing anyway.
It's the shift that happened inside us.
The faith that got stretched.
The God who showed up anyway.

Reflect

Think back to a moment that didn't turn out how you hoped. Can you see even a glimpse of how God might've been protecting or redirecting you? What truth can you speak over that memory now, even if the "why" still isn't clear?

Faith Step

If something you prayed for fell apart, ask yourself—did it leave you broken, or did it set you free? Sometimes what feels like a breakdown is really a breakthrough in disguise.

_____

_____

_____

_____

_____

_____

_____

Prayer

God, I thought this was the right thing. And maybe it was. But now we're hurting. We feel broken, confused, and worn out. Still, I trust that You saw what we couldn't. That You led us for a reason. And that what we walked through is not wasted. Restore what was shaken. Redeem what we don't understand. And keep leading us—one peaceful step at a time. Amen.

You're not falling apart —you're being held together by the One who never lets go.

"Be still, and know that I am God." – Psalm 46:10 NIV

I don't even have the energy to cry anymore. I've cried every day for weeks. And now? I just feel... numb. This season has stripped so much from us—emotionally, mentally, spiritually. It's like we walked into what we thought was obedience and came out on the other side not even recognizing ourselves.
I know my husband is hurting. I see it—the way this broke something in him. Something he was good at. Something he loved. He feels like he's failed himself, the company, and our family... even though, let's be real, our kids didn't even want the move in the first place! Ha! (Pretty sure they made that clear.)
But somehow, the enemy twists it, making him feel like he let everyone down anyway. And if I'm being honest? I've fought those same lies—that maybe this somehow reflects our faith or our strength, too.
But deep down, I know the truth—that's a lie.
A loud, cruel lie.
Because even if this crushed us, it didn't kill us.
Even if we couldn't stay, we still walked through it with prayer, obedience, and hearts wide open to whatever God wanted to do.

Was it about meeting someone who needed him?
Learning to rely fully on God's provision?
Facing fears that were bigger than finances?
Maybe. Maybe not.
And honestly... does.it.even.matter?
I'm so guilty sometimes of trying to find the "purpose"
or the "positive" in everything that I miss the miracle
that's right in front of me. My husband is home. He's
here. We're together. And that's enough.
Right now, none of the questions are worth the
stress. None of them change the ache of this moment.
None of them settle the unease or fix the fallout.
So here's what I'm doing instead:
I'm letting go of trying to understand the purpose—and
starting to ask God to heal the places that are still
hurting.
I'm quitting the need to figure it all out—and giving
myself permission to just be here.
Numb.
Tired.
Still breathing.
Because maybe that's the purpose right now.
Not the answers.
Not the "aha" moment.
Just letting God hold me.

Reflect

Have you been chasing answers in a season that only needs rest? What questions are you holding onto that God may be asking you to lay down—for now?

Faith Step

Let go of one "why" you've been trying to figure out. Write it down, then physically toss or tear up the paper as a symbol of surrender. Say, "God, I don't need to know why. I just need to know You're still with me."

_____

_____

_____

_____

_____

_____

_____

Prayer

God, I'm tired. I'm numb. And I feel like I've lost something I can't quite name. But I know You see the whole picture, and I don't have to chase answers to find peace. Let me rest in You while You do what only You can. Heal the parts of me that feel too broken to fix. I trust You, even when nothing makes sense. Amen.

Crash Landing

"Come to me, all you who are weary and burdened, and I will give you rest." Matthew 11:28 NIV

There were moments in this journey where I felt like I was being pulled in a thousand emotional directions—all at once. Grief. Guilt. Confusion. Exhaustion. It felt like I was flying through the ups and downs, holding it together... until everything hit me at once. It was a crash landing. A collision of everything I'd been carrying at the same time.

One second I'm calm, the next I'm crushed. One minute I'm thinking clearly, the next I'm wondering if I somehow ruined everything.

And now... we had to tell the kids. Not because we thought they'd be upset—honestly, we knew they'd be relieved. Excited, even. But we wanted them to hear our hearts. We wanted them to understand the why behind the shift. Not just the decision, but the faith it took to make it.

Here's what I keep coming back to: you can have big faith and still feel heavy—and that's okay.

God never asked us to keep it together while everything was falling apart. God isn't the author of confusion. He's not the One who causes the pain. But He will use it to teach us how to lean into Him—and that's what I hope our kids have seen.

I hope they saw us trying.
I hope they saw us praying.
I hope they saw us leaning on God when we couldn't stand on our own.
And I pray that when we talk about this season, we don't just share what happened—we share what we've learned.
That sometimes walking away isn't quitting—it's protecting what matters most.
And I just want him back. Not just physically, but emotionally. Spiritually. Joyfully. I want us back. And I believe God is already working on that.
We didn't crash because we failed.
We crash-landed because we tried.
Because we trusted.
And even in the wreckage of emotions, God is already rebuilding.
We're still standing—bruised, yes. But not broken.

Reflect

What emotion are you carrying that you haven't let God into yet? Where do you need to be more honest—with yourself or with someone you love—about how this season has affected you?

Faith Step

Think about someone in your life—your child, your spouse, a friend—who needs to hear truth and tenderness right now. Write down what you want them to know about how this season shaped your heart. Don't sugarcoat it. Don't sermonize it. Just speak from love.

_____

_____

_____

_____

_____

_____

_____

_____

Prayer

Lord, help us to be honest—with our kids, with each other, with ourselves. This season has been hard, and we're tired of pretending it hasn't been. But You've walked with us through it all. Let Your presence guide every conversation. Give us courage to speak truth, and grace to receive it. Heal what's been bruised, and bring peace back into our home. Amen.

The Ride I Didn't Take

"In their hearts humans plan their course, but the Lord establishes their steps." Proverbs 16:9 NIV

I turned down a free trip to Cancun.
You did what?! I hear you...
At the time, I didn't really know what life was going to look like. It was one of those gut feelings I couldn't explain—the kind that whispered, "Say no," even though everything in me wanted to say yes. It didn't make sense. It was a reward I had earned. It was beautiful and exciting and should've been an easy decision. But something deep down told me not to go.
Fast forward to the day my husband quit and was on his way home. The day all the emotions hit harder than I could've prepared for. That same day? It would've been the exact day I would have arrived in Cancun. Alone. On a beach. In another country. While real life needed me here more than ever.
And in that moment, I knew: God knew. He always knew. He was protecting me in advance. That "gut instinct" I felt back in February?
It wasn't hesitation.
It was discernment.
It was God gently saying, "This isn't your assignment. Not this time. Stay close."

And I'm learning—maybe the hard way—that not every opportunity is meant to be taken. Sometimes, God closes a door we were never meant to walk through. Not because it wasn't good, but because it wasn't ours. Not for this season. Not for this calling. Not for the story He's still writing.

We keep asking what the purpose was in all of this. Why we had to walk through so much uncertainty, so many emotions, so many steps we didn't understand. And maybe... maybe it was never about finding some big dramatic "why." Maybe it was about building trust. Maybe it was about sharpening discernment. Maybe it was about learning that obedience now protects you later.

Not every assignment is meant to last forever. And even the ones that look good on the surface can still come with expiration dates. When a door closes, it doesn't mean the story's over. It just means a better one is on the way. And it might just lead straight back to the original plan God had all along.

Reflect

Have you ever said no to something that didn't make sense at the time but later revealed God's protection? What might God be guiding you away from for your good?

Faith Step

Take a moment today to thank God for the closed doors in your life. Even the ones that stung. Even the ones you didn't understand. Ask Him to increase your discernment and to help you trust the "no" just as much as the "yes."

_____

_____

_____

_____

_____

_____

_____

Prayer

Father, thank You for knowing what I don't. For protecting me even when I didn't realize I needed it. For guiding my steps with more care than I ever could on my own. Help me to trust that every no has a purpose, every delay is divine, and every closed door is a step toward something greater. I surrender my plans to You, and I choose to follow where You lead. Amen.

The Coaster Slows, but Faith Grows

You will go out in joy and be led forth in peace..."
Isaiah 55:12a NIV

When we stepped into this season, it felt like that first giant climb on a rollercoaster—hopeful, nervous, excited, terrified.

And now, somehow—after the tears, the tension, the wrestling, the unknown—we're stepping out of it... with peace.

The coaster has slowed, but our faith? It's stronger than ever.

That doesn't make sense on paper.

But that's the thing about walking with God—peace isn't tied to the outcome. It's tied to the obedience.

And the best part? Our kids got to see it all unfold. The excitement on their faces when we told them—it was like this collective breath we didn't even realize we'd been holding finally exhaled.

It reminded me that while this journey has been hard, it hasn't been wasted.

We may have ended up back where we started in a practical sense, but we are NOT the same people who climbed into this ride.

We grew. We trusted. We obeyed—even when it hurt.

And our kids watched us step into something scary, sit in the uneasy, and still choose to follow where we believed God was leading.

That matters.

No, this isn't a "wrap it up with a bow" kind of ending.
But it's not defeat either.
It's faith in motion.
It's proof that stepping into the unknown—even when
it doesn't work out the way you expected—still builds
something eternal.
It strengthens.
It plants seeds.
It changes the whole vibe in your house!
And I don't believe for one second that God is
standing over us saying, "Told you so."
No, I believe He's smiling and saying, "I'm proud of you.
You did the hard thing. And I'm not finished yet."

Reflect

When was the last time you obeyed God even when it didn't lead where you thought it would? What did peace look like on the other side?

Faith Step

Celebrate the peace you've found after a tough decision —even if the result didn't go as planned. Thank God for leading you through it and ask Him to show your kids (or others around you) what obedience looks like in motion.

_____

_____

_____

_____

_____

_____

_____

_____

Prayer

God, thank You for peace on both ends—for being in the decision and the aftermath. Thank You for showing our family what obedience looks like, even when it's hard and messy. Help us see that nothing is wasted with You. Let our children remember that we chose faith over fear, even when it was scary. And as we wait for what's next, help us do so with peace, patience, and full trust in You. Amen.

Riding It Out, Writing It Down

Write down the revelation and make it plain on tablets so that a
herald may run with it." Habakkuk 2:2 NIV

I'm so proud of myself for documenting this whole
thing. Not out of pride in my own strength, but in
what God has done through me. Because this
season? Whew. It wasn't one I would've chosen. It
was a season of emotional whiplash, where fear and
faith fought for the seat beside me, and everything in
me was screaming, "Get off the ride!!"
But, I showed up.
I opened my heart.
And I wrote.
Even when I was exhausted. Even when I had no
words—just a lot of tears, some ugly cries, and the
occasional "Seriously, God?!" moments.
Side note: Can we just appreciate the fact that this is
a 30-day devotional and not 5 weeks? I don't know if
I had anymore days in me. HA!
There were days I had nothing to give—for myself, for
my family, for this devotional. Days I couldn't see how
any of this could possibly be used for good. But still, I
showed up.
This isn't just a journal.
It's not just a devotional.
This is a living, breathing testimony of what it looks
like to hold on through the highs and lows, to stay on
the track when the freefall hits, and to let God write
the story.

I didn't miss the moment.
I didn't bury it or block it out or wish it away (Lord knows I tried)—I documented it.
And now? I have proof that God was in every detail. Even the hard ones.
One day, someone else is going to face a season that looks a lot like this one.
And when they do, they're going to read these words and realize they're not crazy.
They're not broken.
They're not faithless.
They're just in the middle of their story.
And now? I get to be the reminder that God shows up in the middle—even when it feels like the wheels are coming off.
So yes—I'm proud.
Because what I've created here? It's ministry. It's obedience. It's transformation documented in real time.
Look what God let me write.

Reflect

What moments of your story are worth documenting right now—even if they're messy or unfinished?

Faith Step

Thank God for the courage to show up in your own story. Take time to reread something you've written—whether it's one sentence or one page—and praise Him for being present in it.

_____

_____

_____

_____

_____

_____

_____

_____

Prayer

God, thank You for inviting me to co-write this story with You. Thank You for giving me the courage to show up and put words to the hardest season of my life. Use it to speak to someone else when they need it most. I pray that every entry, every tear, and every praise in these pages points straight back to You. This is Your story, Lord—and I'm honored You let me be part of it. Amen.

You're not behind.
You're not disqualified.
You're exactly where
you're meant to be.

Off Track, On Purpose

Write down the revelation and make it plain on tablets so that a
herald may run with it." Habakkuk 2:2 NIV

I wish I could say we have clarity. That we know
exactly why God had my husband in Dothan for 5
weeks. But the truth is... we don't. In fact, we have
more questions now than we did at the beginning.
But one thing I've learned is this: sometimes it's not
about the destination—it's about the detour. And even
the detours we never asked for can still lead us
straight into God's purpose. They may not come with
clear signs or perfect explanations, but they come
with something better: His presence.
Because when God asks you to take a step, He
doesn't require you to understand the outcome. He
just asks for obedience. Sometimes that one step is
what opens the next door. And if we never take the
step... we may never see what was waiting.
Maybe you've missed your step before.
Maybe you're sitting in the tension of wondering if
you got it wrong. Can I just say?
This might be your sign to ask God for another
chance. Because He's not sitting up in heaven shaking
His head saying, "Good grief, can't you just get it?"
He's waiting. Patiently. Because He knows the whole
picture. There is purpose in the process—even the
parts that feel pointless to us.

When this journey began, I was just trying to process everything.
The emotions.
The weight of the unknown.
The tension between peace and panic.
I started journaling because it was the only thing that made me feel grounded. And all I could ask was, "Why Dothan?"
And the only answer I've found is this: it was never meant to be permanent. But it was packed with purpose.
Maybe the purpose wasn't about what we were stepping into.
Maybe it was about what God was growing in us through it.
Maybe it wasn't about arriving—it was about strengthening our faith with every awkward step.
And that alone? Is enough for me to keep trusting Him with what comes next.

Reflect

Where have you been hoping for clarity but instead received growth? Can you look back and see how God was working—even in the places that still don't fully make sense?

Faith Step

Write down one area where you're still waiting on answers. Then ask God to shift your perspective: "Lord, help me stop searching for reasons and start trusting You with the purpose." Circle it. Date it. Trust Him to move—even if it's behind the scenes.

_____

_____

_____

_____

_____

_____

_____

_____

Prayer

God, I may not have the clarity I hoped for, but I trust You haven't wasted a moment of this journey. Thank You for meeting me in the unknown and reminding me that obedience is never wasted. Help me release the need for answers and rest in knowing You're still writing this story. Give me peace and courage to keep walking. In Jesus' name, Amen.

final word!
for such a time as this...

If you made it to the last page, let me just say this: I'm proud of you.

Whether you journaled your heart out or just read quietly and cried in silence... whether you skipped days or devoured them all in one sitting... whether this was a hard season, a healing one, or both—you made it here.

And maybe you're still waiting for the "why."

Maybe you're still wondering what God is doing.

But maybe, just maybe, you're already living the miracle.

Because even when the outcome didn't make sense, you showed up. You leaned in. You let God speak.

So keep listening.
Keep trusting.
Keep writing.
Keep walking.

Because this ride may have had some drops, but it's not the end.

God's just getting started.

xoxo
alicia

"And who knows whether you have not come to the kingdom for such a time as this?"

ESTHER 4:14 ESV

"Being confident of this, that He who began a good work in you will carry it on to completion until the day of Christ Jesus."

PHILIPPIANS 1:6 NIV

A sign of completion and a new beginning.

FROM THE FIRST 7 TO THE FINAL 7
APRIL 11, 2024 –
THE 7 THAT SPARKED MY SURRENDER.
APRIL 15, 2025 –
THE 7 THAT MARKED MY BREAKTHROUGH.
PAY ATTENTION TO HIS SIGNS. THEY MATTER.

www.ingramcontent.com/pod-product-compliance
Lightning Source LLC
Chambersburg PA
CBHW051317120626
46547CB00015B/2276